FAVOURITE
BARBECUE
RECIPES

*Compiled by
Simon Haseltine*

SALMON

INDEX

These recipes provide guidelines only regarding cooking times. However, actual cooking times will vary depending on whether you use an exterior electric grill, charcoal or gas BBQ, if your BBQ has a lid, as well as the thickness of the food you are cooking. Please ensure that your food is piping hot and cooked through at all times.

Cover picture photograph © Istvan Bacs / Alamy Stock Photo
Back cover and title page photograph © David Noton Photography / Alamy Stock Photo
Printed and published by J. Salmon Ltd. © Copyright

STEAK KEBABS WITH SATAY SAUCE

750g rump steak   2 tablespoons soy sauce
1 tablespoon honey   1 teaspoon ground ginger
2 teaspoons cornflour mixed with a splash of water
6 wooden skewers (pre-soaked)
Satay Sauce:
100g roasted peanuts (unsalted)   1 red onion (chopped)
1 clove garlic (crushed)   25g butter (unsalted)
1 teaspoon curry powder   1 teaspoon chilli flakes
1 tablespoon soy sauce   250ml water

Cut the steak into bite-sized pieces. Combine all the other ingredients in a large bowl and add the steak. Place in the fridge to marinate for 2 hours. Thread the steak onto the skewers and BBQ for around 5 to 10 minutes. Baste with any remaining marinade and turn regularly, until cooked through. Serve with the satay sauce. Serves 6.

To make the Satay Sauce: Blend the peanuts in a food processor. Sauté the onion and garlic in the butter for 10 minutes, then stir in the curry powder, chilli flakes, soy sauce and ground peanuts. Stir for a few minutes, then add the water. Bring to the boil and simmer for 10 to 15 minutes until the sauce has thickened. Serve on the steak kebabs.

CHILLI BURGERS

400g minced beef
1 red onion (finely chopped)
2 green chilli peppers (chopped – seeds removed)
1 teaspoon dried mixed herbs
1 egg (beaten)
1 small tin kidney beans (drained and lightly mashed)
1 tablespoon tomato ketchup
4 tablespoons breadcrumbs
Salt and pepper (to season)

In a large bowl, combine all the ingredients together, using wet hands to ensure they are fully mixed. Season with salt and pepper. Divide into 4 beef burger shaped patties, wrap in clingfilm and chill for an hour or more. Grill over the BBQ for 10 minutes each side or until fully cooked through. Serve in a burger bun with salad and a dash of chilli sauce. Serves 4.

SPIT ROAST CHICKEN

2 tablespoons dark soy sauce   1 chicken
1 tablespoon olive oil   100g butter
1 lemon (zest and juice)   2 tablespoons fresh tarragon (chopped)
Salt and pepper (to season)

Ensure your BBQ has a spit roast attachment and if cooking on charcoal, allow the flames to die down and the coals to glow red. Mix together the soy sauce, olive oil and lemon juice and rub over the chicken, then cover and leave to marinate in the fridge for 2 hours. Skewer the chicken onto the spit and rake away the coals (if cooking over charcoal) directly from under the chicken, to avoid any flare ups from the dripping fat. Melt the butter in a pan and stir in the tarragon and lemon zest, plus a little salt and pepper to season. Cook the chicken for around 2 hours with the lid closed, basting with the tarragon butter every 30 minutes. Check that the chicken is fully cooked by testing if the juices run clear. Leave to rest for 20 minutes before serving. Serves 4 to 6 (depending on size of chicken).

STUFFED SAUSAGES

8 pork and apple sausages
English mustard
24 prunes
8 smoked bacon rashers
8 wooden cocktail sticks (pre-soaked)

Prick the sausages, then bring to the boil and simmer for 10 minutes. Remove from the heat, drain and allow to cool. Next, cut a slit in each sausage and spread a little English mustard along each one. Place 3 prunes in each and wrap a bacon rasher around the sausage. Secure with a cocktail stick and place over the BBQ for around 10 minutes or until cooked though. Serves 4.

ROSEMARY LAMB CHOPS

1 lemon (zest and juice)
2 cloves garlic (crushed)
1 tablespoon mango chutney
50ml olive oil   Pinch chilli flakes
1 heaped tablespoon rosemary (chopped)
1 heaped tablespoon parsley (chopped)
4 lamb chops
Freshly ground black pepper

Place all the ingredients (apart from the lamb chops and black pepper) in a large bowl and mix together. Add the lamb chops and rub the marinade all over. Cover and place in the fridge for a few hours. Remove the chops from the bowl and sprinkle with some freshly ground black pepper and place over the BBQ. Cook, turning frequently and basting with any remaining marinade for around 10 minutes or until cooked to your liking. Serves 4.

POSH FISH CAKES

1 red onion (finely chopped)	500g mashed potato
Knob butter	1 tablespoon dill (chopped)
250g smoked salmon fillets	A little flour (for dusting)
250g smoked haddock fillets	1 egg (beaten)
350ml white wine	1 cup fresh breadcrumbs

Place the onion and butter in a frying pan and cook for 5 minutes until softened. Add the fish fillets and wine, stir, cover, and simmer for a further 5 minutes. Remove from the heat and cool, then strain out the wine (discard or use as a sauce) and flake the fish. Mix together the onion, flaked fish, mashed potato and dill in a large bowl, then form into 8 cakes. Dust each fish cake with flour, then dip into the beaten egg and coat with breadcrumbs. Chill for an hour, then cook over the BBQ for 5 minutes each side or until cooked through. Makes 8 fish cakes.

PORK AND APPLE SKEWERS

4 pork medallions   2 cooking apples
10 wooden skewers (pre-soaked)
Marinade:
1 tablespoon honey
1 tablespoon soft brown sugar
2 tablespoons soy sauce
1 tablespoon chilli sauce
1 lemon (zest and juice)

Place all the marinade ingredients (except the lemon juice) into a bowl and mix well. Cut the pork medallions into long, thin strips and add to the marinade, coat well. Leave to marinate in the fridge for a few hours. When you are ready to cook, remove the core from the apples and cut into chunks, then drizzle over the lemon juice. Thread the pork strips onto the skewers, together with the apple chunks, then brush over any remaining marinade. Place over the BBQ for around 10 minutes, turning regularly, until the pork is cooked thoroughly. Makes 10 skewers.

HOT CHICKEN WINGS

18 chicken wings
200ml oil
4 cloves garlic (crushed)
1 tablespoon smoked paprika

1 tablespoon chilli powder
1 tablespoon curry powder
1 teaspoon chilli flakes
1 lime (zest and juice)

Score the chicken wings through the skin. Combine all the remaining ingredients in a bowl and add the chicken wings. Mix together well, cover and refrigerate overnight. Cook over the BBQ for 10 minutes until browned all over and cooked through. Serve warm or cold. Makes 18 portions.

STEAK WRAPS

1 pack tortilla wraps	**Salt and pepper (to season)**
4 sirloin steaks	**1 jar salsa**
Splash olive oil	**1 tub crème fraîche**

Cut each tortilla wrap in half with a sharp knife and place over the BBQ for a few moments to warm through. Meanwhile, brush each steak with a little oil and season with salt and pepper. Place over the BBQ for around 10 minutes, turning once, until cooked to your liking. Remove from the heat and allow to rest for 5 minutes, then slice into small strips. Place a dollop of salsa and crème fraîche onto each wrap and layer over the steak slices. Serve warm with a green salad. Makes 6 wraps.

CHILLI CHICKEN PITTAS

1kg pack chicken thighs (skinned, boned and chopped into bite-sized pieces)
8 wooden skewers (pre-soaked)
1 pack pitta breads   1 jar salsa
Marinade:
3 cloves garlic (crushed)
100ml chilli sauce
100ml natural yoghurt
1 lemon (zest and juice)

Place all the marinade ingredients into a large bowl and mix well. Add the chicken pieces, cover and chill for a few hours. Thread the chicken pieces onto the skewers and brush with any remaining marinade. Cook over the BBQ for around 10 to 15 minutes until cooked thoroughly. Serve inside pitta breads, with a salad and a dollop of salsa. Makes 8 pittas.

GRILLED SARDINES

6 fresh sardines (or mackerel)	1 tomato (finely chopped)
150g fresh breadcrumbs	Handful basil leaves (finely chopped)
½ pepper (finely chopped)	Salt and pepper (to season)
Pinch cayenne pepper	1 lemon (juice)

Remove the head from the sardines, then cut open along the belly from the head end to the tail and remove the innards with your finger. Wash the fish thoroughly and dry with kitchen paper. Make the stuffing by mixing together the breadcrumbs, pepper, cayenne pepper, tomato, basil and season with salt and pepper. Add a teaspoon of water if required then spoon the stuffing into each fish. Place the fish in a fish rack, drizzle with the lemon juice and cook over the BBQ for 5 minutes each side. Serves 6.

BOOZY ORANGE GAMMON WITH APPLE GLAZE

4 tablespoons marmalade (thick cut)   2 tablespoons French dressing
1 tablespoon white wine   6 gammon slices (thick)
Apple Glaze:
25g butter   2 eating apples (sliced)
1 tablespoon honey   1 tablespoon golden syrup
1 lemon (juice)   100ml apple juice   1 tablespoon brandy

Combine the marmalade, French dressing and wine in a pan for a few minutes and cook gently until the marmalade has melted. Remove from the heat and pour over the gammon steaks, cover and marinate in the fridge for a few hours. BBQ the gammon for 10 minutes, turning once until cooked through. Remove from the heat and top with the glazed apples just before serving.

To make the Apple Glaze: Heat the butter gently in a frying pan, then add the apple and cook for around 10 minutes until caramelised. Remove the apples from the pan and add the remaining ingredients to the butter and simmer for a few minutes until the glaze has thickened. Return the apples and top each gammon steak prior to serving. Serves 6.

BARBECUED STUFFED TROUT

4 trout
Stuffing:
2 rashers smoked bacon (chopped)
30g pine nuts
1 red onion (finely chopped)
300g dried breadcrumbs
100g sour cream
4 spring onions (shredded)

Gut and trim the fins from the fish and clean thoroughly. Fry the bacon and pine nuts together for 5 minutes, then make the stuffing by mixing with the red onion, breadcrumbs and sour cream. Fill the cavity of each fish with the stuffing. Place each fish on a greased double layer of kitchen foil and sprinkle over the spring onions. Fold over the foil to form 4 parcels, then place over the BBQ for around 15 minutes (depending on the size of the fish), or until cooked through. Serves 4.

SWEET AND SOUR SPARE RIBS

12 pork spare ribs
Marinade:
2 tablespoons soy sauce   2 tablespoons soft brown sugar
1 teaspoon ground ginger   2 tablespoons white wine vinegar
4 tablespoons tomato ketchup   4 spring onions (chopped)
1 tablespoon hoisin sauce   1 teaspoon chilli flakes

Mix together all the marinade ingredients in a large bowl. Add the spare ribs, rub the marinade all over, then cover and chill for a few hours in the fridge or overnight. Cook over the BBQ for 10 to 15 minutes (depending on thickness), turning once and baste with any remaining marinade. Serves 6.

SEAFOOD SKEWERS

18 king prawns   12 scallops (halved)
1 tin smoked oysters   2 limes (cut into wedges)
6 wooden skewers (pre-soaked)   2 limes (juice)
Anchovy Butter:
250g butter (unsalted and softened)
45g tin anchovy fillets (drained)
1 clove garlic (crushed)   Pinch chilli flakes
½ lime (juice)

Peel and devein the prawns (if necessary) but leave the tails intact. Thread the prawns, scallops, oysters and lime wedges onto the skewers and then drizzle over the lime juice. Place over the BBQ and cook for around 5 minutes, turning regularly, until cooked through. Serve with the anchovy butter. Serves 6.

To make the Anchovy Butter: Beat together all the ingredients and chill before serving with the seafood skewers.

CHICKEN FILLETS WITH BASIL BUTTER

4 chicken breast fillets (skin on)
Handful basil leaves (finely chopped)
1 clove garlic (crushed)
1 tablespoon pine nuts (toasted and chopped)
1 tablespoon parmesan cheese (grated)
150g butter (softened)

Place the chicken fillets on a plate. Mix together the basil, garlic, pine nuts and parmesan cheese. Spread a little of the butter under the skin of each fillet. Place the fillets over the BBQ and baste frequently with the remaining butter. Cook for 15 minutes, turning once, until cooked through. Serves 4.

GRILLED SALMON FILLETS

50ml soy sauce	1 lime (zest and juice)
30ml sherry	4 salmon fillets
1 tablespoon honey	20 cherry tomatoes

Place the marinade ingredients (excluding the cherry tomatoes) into a large bowl and mix well. Add the salmon fillets, coat evenly, then cover and marinate in the fridge for a few hours. Next, place the salmon and cherry tomatoes over the BBQ with the fish skin side down, brush with any remaining marinade and cook for 5 minutes, turning once, until cooked through. Serve the salmon with home cooked chips and the grilled cherry tomatoes. Serves 4.

HERBY MEATBALL LOLLYPOPS

100g sausage meat	1 tablespoon mixed herbs
100g beef mince	Pinch chilli flakes
100g breadcrumbs	1 egg (beaten)
1 onion (finely chopped)	Oil
12 cocktail sticks (pre-soaked)	

Place the sausage meat and beef mince in a bowl, together with the breadcrumbs, onion, herbs, chilli flakes and egg and mix well with wet hands. Form the mixture into 12 even-sized tight balls and insert a cocktail stick in each. Brush with oil and cook over the BBQ for around 10 minutes until brown and cooked through. Serves 6.

BBQ LEG OF LAMB

1 leg of lamb   **Pinch chilli flakes**
100ml olive oil   **2 sprigs rosemary (leaves only)**
4 cloves garlic (crushed)   **1 lemon (zest and juice)**
Salt and pepper (to season)

Ask your butcher to bone the leg of lamb and butterfly it. Place the lamb in a bowl with the olive oil, garlic, chilli flakes, rosemary leaves, lemon zest and juice, season well and rub the marinade all over. Cover and leave in the fridge overnight. The following day, place the lamb over the BBQ and cook for 15 minutes each side (slightly less for pink), basting with any remaining marinade. Once cooked, remove from the BBQ to a serving plate and leave to rest for 10 minutes before serving. Serves 6.

HOMEMADE MAYONNAISE

2 eggs (yolks only)	**100ml extra virgin olive oil**
1 teaspoon Dijon mustard	**1 teaspoon lemon juice**
100ml sunflower oil	**Salt and pepper (to season)**

Using an electric whisk, beat the egg yolks and mustard together. Gently add both oils, a little at a time beating continuously until smooth and creamy. Next, whisk in the lemon juice and season to taste. Store in the fridge but eat within 2 days.

To make Chilli Mayonnaise: Add a pinch of chilli powder (or to taste).

To make Garlic Mayonnaise: Add 2 crushed garlic cloves and a pinch of dried herbs. Makes 200ml.

CHUNKY TOMATO KETCHUP

1 red onion (finely chopped)
1 stick celery (chopped)
Oil
2 cloves garlic (crushed)
2 tins chopped tomatoes

1 tablespoon tomato purée
3 tablespoons caster sugar
Pinch dried mixed herbs
150ml red wine vinegar
Salt and pepper (to season)

Sauté the onion and celery in a little oil for 10 minutes until the onion has softened. Add the garlic and sauté for a further few minutes. Next add the chopped tomatoes, tomato purée, sugar, herbs, and vinegar and bring to the boil. Reduce the heat and simmer for 25 minutes or until the ketchup has thickened. Season to taste. Pour into sterilised jars, label and allow to cool. Store in the fridge but use within 3 weeks. Makes 200ml.

To make Chilli Tomato Sauce: Take 6 tablespoons of ketchup and stir through 1 chopped red chilli and a pinch of smoked paprika.

BBQ VEGETABLE STACKS

1 aubergine (sliced)
1 beef tomato (sliced)
2 mozzarella cheese balls (sliced)
Olive oil

4 large field mushrooms
Splash soy sauce
Pinch chilli flakes
1 jar pesto

Salt and pepper (to season)

Cut the aubergine into 8 thick slices, and cut the beef tomato and mozzarella cheese into 4 slices. Brush a little olive oil on the aubergine and tomato slices, place over the BBQ to grill for 2 minutes each side, then remove from the heat. Meanwhile, place the mushrooms on a double layer of kitchen foil, drizzle with a little soy sauce, olive oil and a sprinkle of chilli flakes, then fold the foil to form 4 parcels. Place the parcels over the BBQ for 10 minutes, then remove from the heat. Open the foil and top each mushroom with 2 slices of the cooked aubergine, a slice of tomato and a slice of mozzarella cheese. Season with salt and pepper to taste. Place back (do not close up the foil) over the BBQ to warm through for 5 minutes, then remove to a serving plate and top each vegetable stack with a dollop of pesto and serve. Serves 4.

CHEESY CORN ON THE COBS

100g Stilton cheese (grated or crumbled)
100g mature Cheddar cheese (grated)
100ml Greek yoghurt
1 teaspoon mustard flour
Sea salt (to season)
4 corn cobs (in their leafy husks)
4 knobs butter

Place the cheeses in a bowl and then beat in the Greek yoghurt and mustard flour until smooth. Season with a little sea salt and chill in the refrigerator. Meanwhile, wrap each corn cob in a double layer of kitchen foil and cook over the BBQ for around 20 minutes, turning a few times. When cooked, carefully unwrap the foil and husk from each cob (beware of the steam), add a knob of butter to each corn, sprinkle with additional salt, and serve with a dollop of the cheese dressing. Serves 4.

CHILLI BBQ BEANS

Knob butter   2 red onions (chopped)
2 cloves garlic (crushed)
1 red and 1 green pepper (deseeded and chopped)
2 tins mixed beans in tomato sauce
2 tins chopped tomatoes   100g tomato ketchup
2 teaspoons chilli flakes (or to taste)
200ml water

Melt the butter in a frying pan and sauté the onion and garlic for 10 minutes until softened. Add the peppers and sauté for a few more minutes, then add the mixed beans, chopped tomatoes, ketchup, chilli flakes and water, stir and simmer for 30 minutes until reduced and thickened. Pour into a heavy based pan and keep warm on the side of the BBQ prior to serving. Serves 4.

CURRIED VEGETABLE BURGERS

Small tin cannellini beans (drained)
1 carrot (grated)   1 courgette (grated)
1 red onion (finely chopped)
4 spring onions (finely chopped)
Handful spinach (finely chopped)
2 teaspoons curry powder (or more to taste)
Pinch chilli flakes   3 tablespoons flour

In a large bowl, roughly mash the drained cannellini beans, then fold through the remaining ingredients, mixing together with wet hands. Shape into 4 beef burger shaped patties and wrap with clingfilm. Chill for an hour or more. Grill over the BBQ for 10 minutes each side, or until cooked through. Serve in a burger bun with salad and some curry ketchup. Serves 4.

STUFFED JACKET POTATOES

4 jacket size potatoes   **Good handful spinach leaves**
50g butter (softened)   **100g Cheddar cheese (grated)**
4 spring onions

Bake or microwave the potatoes until cooked through. Allow to cool, then cut off the top third from each potato. Scoop out the flesh and mash well with the butter, spinach leaves, cheese and spring onions. Spoon the filling back into each potato and place the top loosely over the mixture. Wrap each potato in a double layer of kitchen foil and place in the BBQ coals for 20 minutes to heat through. Serves 4.

ROASTED ONIONS

4 red onions
1 teaspoon mixed herbs
Pinch chilli flakes
4 teaspoons honey
4 tablespoons balsamic vinegar

Peel each onion and cut into quarters. Place each onion (the 4 quarters) on a double layer of kitchen foil, sprinkle with the herbs and chilli flakes, then drizzle over the honey and balsamic vinegar. Loosely fold the foil over the onion pieces and cook in the embers of a charcoal BBQ for 15 minutes, or over the grill of a gas BBQ for 20 minutes, until the onions are tender. Serves 4.

FRUITY KEBABS

Selection of fruit – around 60 bite-sized pieces in total
(strawberries, raspberries, pineapple, bananas, apricots, plums, peaches, blackberries etc)
1 lemon (juice)
Black pepper
6 wooden skewers (pre-soaked)
4 tablespoons honey
100g milk chocolate (broken into pieces)
Splash double cream

Prepare the fruit and cut into bite-sized pieces, then place in a bowl and drizzle over the lemon juice and a little black pepper. Stir gently then divide the fruit between the 6 skewers and brush with the honey. Put the chocolate pieces and a splash of double cream in a bowl over a pan of hot water to melt. Meanwhile, place the fruit kebabs over the BBQ for around 4 to 5 minutes, turning often, until the honey has caramelised. Stir the melted chocolate and drizzle over each kebab on a serving plate. Serves 6.

VEGETABLE KEBABS

2 red onions (sliced into chunks)
2 courgettes (thickly sliced)
3 peppers (various colours – chunked)
12 small button mushrooms
12 cherry tomatoes
6 wooden skewers (pre-soaked)
Marinade:
2 tablespoons soy sauce
2 tablespoons honey
1 tablespoon balsamic vinegar

Clean and prepare the vegetables, then divide them between the skewers, alternating each piece to make 6 colourful kebabs. Mix together the marinade ingredients, then drizzle evenly over each kebab. Cook over the BBQ for around 10 minutes, turning regularly and basting with any remaining marinade, until cooked all over. Serves 6.

BANANA SPLITS

Knob butter (unsalted and melted for greasing)
6 bananas
1 large bag chocolate buttons (both milk and white)
Small tub double cream
6 teaspoons rum (optional adult version)
1 heaped tablespoon icing sugar

Using a double layer of kitchen foil, brush 6 squares with the melted butter. Cut a slit along the top edge of each banana to half way through the flesh (but leave the skins on) and insert the chocolate buttons, alternating milk and white. Wrap each banana with the foil and place over a gentle BBQ for around 10 minutes (keeping the chocolate buttons upper most). Meanwhile, whip the cream with the rum and a little icing sugar. Open the foil on each serving plate and serve with a large dollop of the whipped cream. Serves 6.

VINE WRAPPED CAMEMBERT

2 vine leaves   **1 clove garlic (sliced)**
1 Camembert   **A few sprigs rosemary**
Selection of crackers

Rinse the vine leaves in cold water, then pat dry with kitchen paper. Take the Camembert cheese and slice off the top crust. Poke the sliced garlic and rosemary sprigs into the cheese then double wrap in the vine leaves. Place over the BBQ for 5 minutes, turning once. Open up the vine leaves and serve with crackers or French toast. Serves 4 as a side dish.

HAWAIIAN PINEAPPLE

1 pineapple   **Black pepper**
6 teaspoons demerara sugar   **Tot rum**

Peel and thickly slice the pineapple into rings, then sprinkle each side with the demerara sugar and a little black pepper. Grill over the BBQ for around 5 minutes, turning once. Remove from the BBQ and drizzle a little rum over each slice and serve with a dollop of thick cream. Serves 6

ELDERFLOWER AND RASPBERRY LEMONADE

200g raspberries (pre-frozen) 1 lemon (juice)
1 tablespoon caster sugar 900ml sparkling water (chilled)
100ml elderflower cordial 1 lemon (sliced)

Using a wooden spoon, push the raspberries through a sieve, collecting the juice in a large jug. It is best to freeze the raspberries first, then thaw them, as they will release more juice. Add the caster sugar, elderflower cordial and lemon juice, then stir until the sugar has dissolved. Add the chilled sparkling water and ice if required, stir and serve with lemon slices immediately. Makes around 1 litre.

CHOCOLATE ORANGES

6 navel oranges
6 teaspoons demerara sugar
6 teaspoons orange liqueur
6 after dinner style chocolate mints
12 cocktail sticks (pre-soaked)

Slice the top third off each orange and poke the flesh downwards with a sharp knife. Sprinkle the flesh with the demerara sugar, then drizzle with a little orange liqueur. Place a chocolate mint on each orange and seal with the lid, securing with a couple of cocktail sticks (snap off the tops). Double wrap in kitchen foil and place in the dying embers of a charcoal BBQ (or on top of the BBQ, turning regularly), for 15 minutes until cooked through. Carefully unwrap and eat the chocolate orange with a spoon. Serves 6.

GINGER APPLES

2 lemons (juice)
100g butter (melted)
4 tablespoons demerara sugar
4 green eating apples
6 tablespoons stem ginger (diced)

Place the lemon juice, butter and demerara sugar into 3 separate bowls. Slice each apple in half and dip the cut side into the lemon juice, then the butter and finally the demerara sugar. Place the apples over the BBQ, cut side down, and cook for around 5 minutes, then turn and cook for a further 5 minutes. Place on a serving plate cut side up, sprinkle with the diced ginger and serve with whipped cream. Serves 6.

METRIC CONVERSIONS

The weights, measures and oven temperatures used in the preceding recipes can be easily converted to their imperial equivalents. The conversions listed below are only approximate, having been rounded up or down as may be appropriate.

Weights

Avoirdupois	Metric
1 oz.	just under 30 grams
4 oz. (¼ lb.)	app. 115 grams
8 oz. (½ lb.)	app. 230 grams
1 lb.	454 grams

Liquid Measures

Imperial	Metric
1 tablespoon (liquid only)	20 millilitres
1 fl. oz.	app. 30 millilitres
1 gill (¼ pt.)	app. 145 millilitres
½ pt.	app. 285 millilitres
1 pt.	app. 570 millilitres
1 qt.	app. 1.140 litres

Oven Temperatures

	°Fahrenheit	Gas Mark	°Celsius
Slow	300	2	150
	325	3	170
Moderate	350	4	180
	375	5	190
	400	6	200
Hot	425	7	220
	450	8	230
	475	9	240

Flour as specified in these recipes refers to plain flour unless otherwise described.

The pictures featured in this book are not intended to illustrate any specific recipe.